JEAN VIL

CHARTRES
AND ITS
CATHEDRAL

94 photos in black and white, and in colour.

Translated by M.-Th. Olano and Ian Robertson

ARTHAUD

In the same collection :

The sights of Carcassonne
Châteaux of the Loire
Châteaux of the Ile-de-France
The sights of Mont-Saint-Michel
Paris
Versailles

LIST OF CAPTIONS

THE EVANGELIST SAINT MARK ON THE SHOULDERS OF THE PROPHET DANIEL (STAINED GLASS).
STAINED GLASS OF THE TREE OF JESSE. LOWER PART. JESSE AND TWO PROPHETS.

THE STAINED GLASS OF THE CALENDAR

51. Sagittarius.
52. The balance.
53. December. Slaughtering swine.
54. Christ.
50. The stained glass of Charlemagne. Joust of Roland and Ferragut.
55. Stained glass windows of the church of Saint-Pierre.
56. Our Lady of the Pillar.

ENCLOSURE OF THE CHOIR

57. The Visitation.
58. The Nativity of the Virgin.
60. The Adoration of the magi.
61. Paving of the nave. The centre of the maze.

ANCIENT ROOD SCREEN

59. The shepherds receive the message.
62. The Nativity.
63. The sleep of the magi and their awakening by the angel.
    To the right their horses leaving the stable.
64. Detail of a bas-relief representing the terrestrial world.
65. Animal and vegetable decoration.
66. A huntsman.

MUSEUM (the former bishop's palace)

67. The italian room.
68, 69. Processional cross and bishop's crook of raised enamel.
70. Coat of mail and helmet.
71. Zurbaran : The holy Lucy.
72. Virgin and child, surrounded by saints.
73. Enamels of Leonard Limosin. The apostles, Saint Simon, Saint
    Bartholomew and Saint James the lesser.
74. Holbein : Portrait of Erasme.
75. Deuret : The hunt of the Duchess of Lorraine.

THE THREE MAGI (STAINED GLASS).

CHARTRES AND ITS CATHEDRAL

Cathedrals contribute as much if not more to the prestige of France as her châteaux. Often related to each other, but nevertheless each quite different, they belong to the landscape of France. There are a few, such as that at Chartres, the presence of which imposes upon a whole district. Noticeable from afar across the flat horizon of Beauce, at first it appears to hang quite alone between fields and clouds, between Heaven and Earth. Then, as one draws closer to its mass, the town can be discerned nestling at its base.

Even if, from time to time, this agglomeration has overflowed into new districts, the town centre, which has been inhabited for over 2,000 years, retains its mediaeval geniality. Its picturesque hillocks and the inconsequential layout of its streets are a pleasant change from obsessional lines and commonplace geometry.

Only an hour from Paris, old Chartres bewitches the visitor with its provincial charm.

THE TOWN'S FORMATION.

When Caesar brought war to the Gauls, Chartres, or rather Autricum. was the main town of the Carnutes, the first tribe to rebel against Rome. Later it took their name; Lutece became Paris likewise, as did almost all the capitals of the various tribes. From Caesar himself we know that yearly assemblies, political and religious at the same time, and presided over by druids, were held in the Carnute country, considered as the centre of an area.

Autricum derived its name from the river Autura, the Eure. This flows first towards the south-east and the Loire, then turns abruptly at right angles before reaching the Seine just above Rouen. It was near this bend, on a slight promontary suitable for defence, that the town was laid out. We do not know the date of its origins, but in the surrounding area the presence of megaliths and prehistoric tools provide proof of a very ancient civilization settled in the region.

In Gallo-Roman times the town, at first grouped on the heights, lay in the perimeter of an almost regular rectangle. Little by little it reached down the slopes as far as the river and even beyond. There was an amphitheatre there. Two aqueducts converged on Autricum and numerous roads radiated from it, which time has not quite obliterated. Caesar's Road, the road to Sens, capital of the province, still exists.

Chartres always was an important road junction and its toponymy is retained in such names as Pontchartrain in the vicinity of Versailles, the streets and gates "chartraines" of Dreux, Evreux and Vendôme.

Cross-road of commerce, stronghold, religious and intellectual centre, such, during the ages, either in turn or simultaneously, are the parts played by Chartres.

COMMERCIAL CROSSROADS, AND STRONGHOLD.

The main towns of the plain of Beauce are situated on its periphery, including Chartres, its capital. Adjoining the Perche, a country of hills, woods and rivers, it has always been, as have the other towns of Beauce, a place of exchanges.

But the era of the barbaric invasions sowed ruins; and likewise fear. The too-exposed valley was evacuated by its inhabitants, who withdrew to the plateau and hastily strengthened their defensive walls, the outline of which can still be followed at the boundary of the upper town. It is marked out by the chevets of Saint-Aignan and the Cathedral, and by the old Cendreuse Gate — which got its name from a ceremony which took place in those days each Ash Wednesday — and by the site of the old castle, which exists no longer (this area is now a covered market).

The county of Chartres, united with those of Blois and Champagne, belonged to powerful nobles, the most famous of whom was Thibault the Cheat. It was acquired by Philippe le Bel in 1286, who incorporated it into the royal domain. Since the reign of Louis XIV, the eldest son of the Duke of Orleans bore the title of Duke of Chartres.

When the shrewd government of Philippe Auguste guaranteed to the royal domain a security previously only prepared by his forebears, the County of Chartres gained from it. The town, which soon became free, then expanded its trade; leather and cloth were worked principally. Again the population extended beyond the old boundaries of the "oppidum" and workshops were set up on both banks of the Eure. They were called the "river trades", besides which mills, driven by hydraulic power, ground into flour the corn of Beauce.

To protect the lower town against possible invaders, new fortifications rose at the end of the 12th century, increasing the length of its surrounding walls to nearly a league (2½ miles). It was in 1356 that an arm of the river was dug out to form a defensive moat on its more vulnerable side. Those ramparts, maintained and strengthened during the Hundred Years War, existed until the last century and are still partially standing, now bordered by encircling boulevards.

If some entrances have for long been obliterated, as have the Cornus Gate (the currier's popular name), the Imboust Gate and the Tire-Veau postern, most of them are still main exits from the circumference

1. LA CATHÉDRALE VUE DU FAUBOURG LA GRAPPE
2. LA ROUTE DE CHARTRES, PRÈS DE CHAMPHOL

2

3

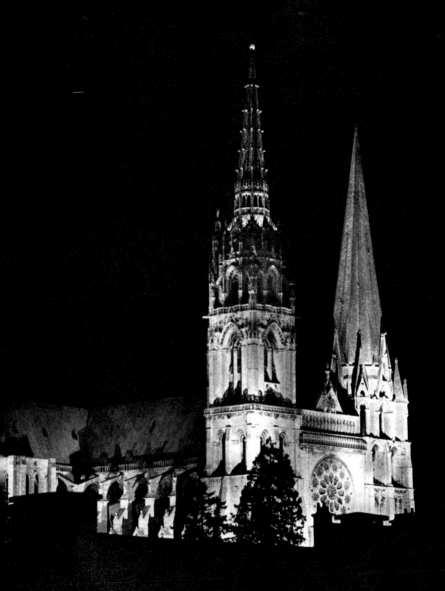

9

10

12 13

PERSPECTIVES VERS LA NEF (12) ET LE CHŒUR (14).
13. ANGLE DU CHŒUR ET DU CROISILLON MÉRIDIONAL

15. DÉAMBULATO
16. COLLATÉRAUX
DU CHŒUR VERS
LE TRANSEPT

17-18. CLOTURE
CHŒUR ET
DÉAMBULATOIRE

of the old town; such as the ancient Gates of Chatelet, Drouaise (towards Dreux) Guillaume, Morard, Saint-Michel and Epars. The latter is even now the centre of traffic. Like most military towns, Chartres had to deny itself open spaces within its fortified belt, and its narrow streets cross and recross each other.

Every time an opposing commander-in-chief intended to starve Paris, he first endeavoured to besiege Chartres, the key to France's granary. The town thus underwent a number of sieges. It was ransacked by Hunald in 743, then by the Normans (of Hastings) in 858; in 911 it saw Rollon retreat.

In May 1360 a siege was raised by a providential storm, " so frightful that it seemed as if the end had come "... "It rained down huge hailstones which killed both mounts and men", thus Froissard reported, and the King of England, Edward III, "gazed towards the church of Chartres" and "promised Our Lady that he would agree to peace". Thus, the Treaty of Brétigny was signed two leagues away.

Chartres fell into the hands of the Anglo-Burgundians in 1417. Its liberation in 1432 was secured thanks to the enterprise of two of its burghers. A cart, apparently laden with baskets of shad, overturned when crossing the drawbridge of Saint Michel Gate, and the men at arms hidden in it easily overpowered the guards in the midst of the confusion brought about by the prepared "accident", while reinforcements were brought up. These were headed by Dunois and other great captains who had served Joan of Arc.

The religious wars brought an army of Huguenots under the walls of Chartres in 1568. They attacked the Drouaise Gate and their artillery had already breached the wall, when quite contrary to expectations, the assaillants melted away. But the struggle did not come to an end, and driven from Paris on the Day of the Barricades (12th May 1588), Henri III came to seek refuge at Chartres. In 1591 Henri of Navarre invested the town. It ignored repeated summonses, but after a strong resistance the inhabitants of Chartres agreed to throw open their gates. The King remembered this, and three years later, as Reims remained in the hands of the League, it was in Chartres Cathedral that he was crowned.

Since then the military history of the town has not been commemorated by any event of importance. As a fortified town it ceased to exist. During the 19th century a great part of its ramparts were pulled down, as well as the castle.

The War of 1870-71 brought the Prussian occupation, and the Beauce was the scene of heavy fighting at Chateaudun, Loigny, and Varize.

19. PORTAIL ROYAL. LE CHRIST EN MAJESTÉ   33

During the 1940 invasion, the young prefect, Jean Moulin, whose name was then little known, opposed brutality with an energetic Resistance. Chartres was bombed slightly at the end of the 1914-1918 war, but suffered from bombardment between 1940 and 1944, particularly on May 26th, 1944, when the Town Hall was badly damaged, and one of the most precious collections of old manuscripts in France was destroyed, together with the library. Finally, on August 15th 1944, began a three day battle for the town. Its liberation preceeded that of Paris by a week only.

THE BIRTHPLACE OF FAMOUS MEN.

It is not only by political and military events that History is made. Before approaching the Spiritual past of Chartres it is as well to mention some of the famous men born there : the poet Philippe Desportes, and his nephew, the noted satirist Mathurin Regnier; the architect and art critic, Felibien; the moralist Pierre Nicole, who retired amongst the recluses of Port-Royal; the Chancellor of France Etienne d'Aligre; the Marquis de Dangeau, one of the few intimates of Louis XIV, and his biographer; Brissot, a member of the Convention; Petion de Ville-neuve, who was Mayor of Paris during the Terror; the humanist, and member of the Convention, Dusaulx; the advocate Chauveau-Lagarde, who pleaded at the trials of Marie-Antoinette and of Charlotte Corday; the engraver Sergent, one of the founders of the French Museum, later to become the Louvre; the actor Fleury; the publisher Hetzel, who also wrote under the name of Stahl; and Marceau, whose anniversary Chartres celebrates faithfully every year; general at twenty-five, he was killed at the height of his career at twenty-seven, after having earned the esteem of his opponents themselves. The base of his statue in the Place des Epars contains some of his ashes.

Chartres also honours by monuments the doctor Noël Ballay, who, born at the nearby village of Fontenay-sur-Eure, was the companion of Brazza; and Louis Pasteur, who tried out his vaccines on sheep from a neighbouring farm at Saint-Germain-la-Gâtine.

A PLACE OF PILGRIMAGE.

Proud of its past, the old city of the Carnutes enjoys world-wide fame on account of its cathedral, but nevertheless the latter cannot be explained outside its historical context. A bishopric since the 4th century, until the reign of Louis XIV Chartres was the head of the largest diocese in France, spreading from the Seine to the Loire and including Saint-Germain-en-Laye and Blois. It was, together with Paris, dependent on the Archbishopric of Sens. Chartres is also a very ancient place of pilgrimage, the origin of which escapes the historian. The legend of the "Virgo paritura", setting down only in the 14th century much earlier beliefs, implied that homage was paid to the Mother of God prior to our era, thanks to the knowledge of the Prophetic texts. During the 16th century the druids were mixed up with this cult.

Chartres won fame as the most ancient christian centre, on account of its martyrs, and reliable texts often refer to the age of its sanctuary. Around the year 876 Charles the Bold donated to Chartres a veil which was considered to have been worn by the Virgin, which the Cathedral still preserves. Charlemagne had received it from the Emperor of Constantinople. It must have been an important reason which caused his grandson to offer one of the most precious relics of the treasury of Aix-la-Chapelle to a church in one of his states. This modest piece of silk has survived to this day through wars and fires, merely being cut down in 1793. The scientific examination to which it has been submitted confirms that it originated in the country and at the time in keeping with tradition.

Bishop Gantelme, during the siege of 911, exposed it on the ramparts, and according to the chroniclers, it was the sight of this that put Rollon to flight.

At the Drouaise Gate an inscription designates the Virgin to be the citizen's protectress, "**Carnutum Tutela**". It was to such protection that the raising of the siege in 1568 was attributed.

Chartres was one of the main objects of pilgrimage during the Middle Ages. Saint Bernard preached the crusade there in 1150, four years after preaching to the great crowds at Vezelay and Spire. One could mention almost all the Kings of France amongst its pilgrims. Saint-Louis came there on foot from Nogent-le-Roi. It was from Paris that Henri III made one of his pilgrimages in 1583, with his queen, and was "worn out, and the soles of his feet were blistered by having trudged so far". Peguy has only revived an old tradition. Nowadays pilgrimages to Chartres have taken on a new look, and the students' pilgrimage is famous.

INTELLECTUAL CENTRE.

The religious history of the town is often bound up with its artistic and intellectual life. Its episcopal Schools were once a beacon to large areas of Europe. St. Fulbert, whose great erudition was gained through his contact with Gerbert — the future Pope Sylvestre II — had so much affection for the schools to which he had given a new life, that he continued to teach after becoming a bishop. His pupils called him "our Socrates". A theologist as well as a philosopher, he was equally able to write verses and to compose music; he corresponded with all the great men of Christendom.

One of his successors, St. Yves of Chartres, imprisoned for a while for reproaching the king on his unlawful marriage, became famous on account of his legal knowledge. Bernard of Chartres, one of the School's chancellors, preached — long before Montaigne — on the value of an enlightened mind rather than cumbersome knowledge, and enjoined attention to the great writers of antiquity, whom he compared to giants on whose shoulders rested those who came after. His brother Thierry, who succeeded the metaphysician Gilbert de la Porrée as chancellor, was interested, as were most of the masters of Chartres, in a multiplicity of problems, including the origin of the Universe. Guillaume de Conches, saturated in the spirit of Cicero and Seneca, became a commentator on Plato.

Research on numbers according to Pythagoras, geometry, the theories of Aristotle handed down by Boëthius, and suchlike topics were those in which the school of Chartres excelled during the 12th century; opposed to the "Cornificiens", it exalted the cult of the intellect. Thus the wisdom of Greece and Rome was implanted in French minds.

John of Salisbury was the last of this succession of humanists; his sharp and subtle mind was shaped by the country's intellectual environment. He became Bishop of Chartres six years after the murder of his friend, the ex-chancellor of England, Thomas à Becket.

Students came from England and even further afield. The School of Paris, and the establishment of the Sorbonne in the 13 th century were to sound the knell for the Schools of Chartres, but their influence lasts in the choice and setting of the subjects sculpted at the portals of the Cathedral.

THE CATHEDRAL

ITS CONSTRUCTION.

Between the 4th century Cathedral and the present one several buildings have succeeded each other. The first Cathedral probably abutted the gallo-roman ramparts. Later on history records various destructions, either accidental, or caused by barbarian raids . It was after that of the Vikings in 858 that Bishop Gislebert had his church reconstructed, of which the crypt of Saint-Lubin still exists. It is situated under the High Altar at the deepest explored level.

Accidentally destroyed by fire in 1020, it was immediately rebuilt by Bishop Fulbert, but on a plan which enveloped the former edifice with its side aisles and ambulatory. Its crypt, the largest in size after that of Saint Peter's in Rome, and Canterbury, was nearly finished by 1024. Saint Fulbert had obtained help from the King of France, Robert II, and even from Canute, the great King of Denmark and England. But he died without seeing his church completed. It was consecrated by Thierry, his successor, on 17th October 1037.

In 1134, in front of the northern aisle, work started on an isolated bell tower, called the New Tower, in spite of it being the most ancient at its foundations and eleven years later the Old Bell Tower began to rise up, as well as the Royal Portal, designed and sculpted for another site than that which it occupies, probably at the rear of the narthex which was connected with the base of both towers. At that time also the side aisles were extended to reach the two towers.

But the 11th century cathedral was not vaulted. Its exceptional width, conceived to shelter the throng of pilgrims — it could hold more than the total population of the town — did not permit any other solution but that the roof should lie directly on the walls.

Another accidental fire occurred on the 10th June 1194, which almost completely destroyed the edifice, nevertheless leaving the façade and towers standing.

Discouraged at first by this catastrophe, which had burnt out one of the most famous churches in Christendom, the inhabitants of Chartres recovered their composure on learning that their relic had narrowly escaped. In fact, immediately the fire started, some clerks, who were anxious to save it, carried it down some stairs — near to the altar — directly connecting the choir and the St. Lubin crypt. They then pulled down the trap door, now wooden, but then iron, according to an eye-witness account. Blocked by the collapse of the building and blazing timber, it still resisted the fire. After two or three days, clearing away the rubble, they found to their delight that the precious object had remained unscathed, together with its rescuers. The papal legate, Cardinal Melior, happening to be present, delivered a stirring address, upon which the Bishop and canons decided to part with some of their wealth "in order to hire workmen worthy of their hire" and its reconstruction was undertaken with enthusiasm.

The town Guilds paid for the stained glass, and thanks to the generosity of high ranking persons, others were to be made. King Philippe Auguste gave a sum of money to cover the cost of eight pillars. A Beauce farmer, with the agreement of his family, gave up his land; a student from London threw in the necklace bought for his fiancée. The building yards were no doubt organised as recorded previously in the texts of 1144 and 1145 : the men were harnessed to wagons which transported enormous blocks of stone from the quarries of Berchères. The distance they had to cover — over seven miles — probably over poor roads, enabled only one journey a day to be made by each cart. One should remember that many of the blocks were over a ton in weight. Church-going does not seem to have been interrupted : pilgrims continued to flock there. Unfortunate quarrels over trivial incidents caused antagonism between the Chapter and the Countess of Chartres' supporters, which had their repercussions as far as the provisional church, where anathemas were hurled! But the building yards continued to work on, regardless. Right from the beginning, in spite of being at war with Philippe Auguste, Richard the Lion Heart authorized those who were collecting for Our Lady of Chartres to circulate throughout England.

The **Book of miracles** written at this time relates astonishing facts : miraculous cures, traffic jams in the cloister caused by the arrival of carts **en masse,** etc. For places, however distant, made their contribution : some gave barrels of wine, others lime or wood for the scaffolding and framework. Pieces of jewelry were sold to benefit the fund. Courville sent beams; Bonneval some lime; and Batilly-en-Gâtinais a dray piled with corn. The men of Château-Landon themselves dragged to Chartres their offering of a load of corn, and the men of Pithiviers did likewise, but, although exhausted, they turned down the help offered by the folk of Puiset, for they were intent on fulfilling their vow to the end. The Bretons of Chartres made it a point of honour only to accept compatriots into their teams for the carriage of masonry.

One of the nicest stories concerns these parishoners of Pithiviers who, sweating, groaning and dog-tired in their harness, stopped to quench their thirst from a pipe of wine held out to them by the villagers of Puiset. So copious were the draughts they drank from the gobelets that the barrel soon sounded hollow. But on shifting it, it still appeared amazingly heavy, much to their surprise. "Having removed the spigot, the pilgrims were to see bright red wine spurt out, of inexpressible fragrance, and a thousand times better than the original. Many who tasted it were immediately cured of numerous illnesses."

While clearing the ruins, a master-builder—who remains unknown—drew up new plans and carried out all necessary calculations of stress and strain. He was assisted by skilled carpenters and stonemasons. Cranes, derricks and winches did not cease to raise the materials higher and higher, and by the end of 1220 the main structures were almost completed, little more than 26 years after the destruction of the old church.

When Saint Louis, still a child, became king, the stained glass was almost in place, and it only remained for the figures in the porches to be sculpted. Then the rood screen was raised — to be pulled down five centuries later — and doubtless for some long time it was hoped that the nine towers originally projected would be built. Its dedication took place in October 1260 — either the 17th or the 24th, the question is debatable.

The Cathedral measured 427 feet in length, internally and its arches stood more than 121 feet above the ground. The width of the main nave is 53 feet (from axis to axis). The internal width is 107 feet, including the side aisles : the internal width of the chancel with both side aisles is 150 feet. With the porches, the transept attains a length of 252 feet. Lastly, the respective heights of the Old and New Bell-Towers (not including the latter's cross) are approximately 338 and 364 feet.

THE CATHEDRAL SINCE THE 13th CENTURY.

Few modifications have taken place since 1260. The 14th century added the high galleries of the lateral façades and the Chapel of Saint Piat, while the 15th century added the Vendome Chapel on the south side. The 16th century's contribution was much more important. It erected the flamboyant spire which so completely transformed the general silhouette of the building ; then came the clock pavilion and the enclosure of the Choir. The decoration of the latter was completed during the following century and into the 18th. From 1757 a succession of changes, which now we can hardly understand, destroyed without scruple several stained glass windows, and disfigured the architectural arrangement of the choir.

The Cathedral was spared the religious wars, and it was hardly damaged during the revolutionary period.

Fire broke out again in 1836, smouldering in the great timber roof, which was called "the forest", destroying it entirely. A metal frame covered by copper replaced it. None of the glass suffered in the intense heat, fanned by the wind for eleven hours over the thick 13th century vaults, which Philippe Auguste's chronicler claimed would last "until the Last Judgement".

Our own times have endeavoured to keep intact this monument, which transcends local values, and is part of the human patrimony. The stained glass was taken down and put under cover in 1918. It was also removed in 1939 and remained undamaged during both wars. The first removal was an occasion to study it in detail.

Too many cathedrals elsewhere have been mutilated by the passing of time; in war or civil war sculptures have been knocked about, statues smashed; by stupidity, dozens of windows have been shattered. Our 20th century is lucky to be able to admire Chartres in its entirety, or nearly so; the most marvellous assembly of images in existence, a collection of stained glass without equal in the world, together with a wealth of carved stone which remains amongst the most remarkable, the spirit of which forms it into the most perfect encyclopedia of christian art.

Besides which, in the history of the architectural quest of the Middle Ages, the solutions of which, bold but unerring, adopted at Chartres, stamp it as the ultimate expression of an era's experience. It also prompted further inspiration.

Erected with enthusiasm, the Cathedral breathes the air of spring. The stones themselves retain their youth. Chartres remains a place of exaltation for believer and aesthete alike.

THE WESTERN FAÇADE AND THE BELL TOWERS.

An assembly of architectural pieces of the finest quality, but of different epochs, this façade of Chartres Cathedral may take one unaware by its general quality of moderation, and its dissymmetry.

Three and a half centuries separate the two spires; one is powerful and unadorned, the other elegantly embellished. From this contrast itself emerges an intense vigour.

For the most part this front belongs to the earlier building : the lower floors of the northern tower, on the left, were commenced in 1134 : the Royal Portal and the three great windows followed in 1145; finally, the Old Bell Tower, on the right, which was built at the same time in one great spurt. In the fire of 1194 this façade only was saved, having just been built.

At about 1200 the floor with the rose-window was added, to finish off the nave which had risen higher than the old one; the vaulting of which, conceived as early as the 12th century, reaching 120 feet from the ground, has attained a record height never attempted before. A modern ten storey building would not reach its apex, and it would.

PORTAIL ROYAL 20. STATUES-COLONNES
                                                    21. ENSEMBLE

22

PORTAIL ROYAL

22. ANNONCIATION, VISITATION, NATIVITÉ, ANNONCE AUX BERGERS, PRÉSENTATION AU TEMPLE

23. VIERGE EN MAJESTÉ   24. ARIST

25. LA MOISSON ET LE CANCER

27. JEUNE ROI

26. DÉTAIL D'UNE COLONNETTE

28. PROPHÈTE (?)   29. LA REINE DE SABA (?) ET SALOMON (?)

PORTAIL NORD

30. JÉRÉMIE, SIMÉO
ET SAINT JEAN-
BAPTISTE
31. ABRAHAM,
MOISE, AARON ET
DAVID
32. ENSEMBLE

34

33

35

36

PORCHE NORD

37

take thirty floors to equal the Old Bell Tower; thirty-two at least to overtop the New Tower.

The Kings' gallery was not erected until after 1250, the same for the main walls of the square stump built over the romanesque tower on the left. Towards 1387, the framework of the spire sheathed in lead was built which was known as the "Lead Bell Tower", or the "New Bell Tower".

This spire was struck by lightning on July 26th 1506. It was then that the services of the "master-builder" Jean Texier, named Jean de Beauce were called upon. After three months of study and planning, he erected in six years, assisted by Thomas le Vasseur, this stone spire, the weight of which necessitated the preliminary placing of buttresses inside the older floors. Work was finished in 1513. Under the rich exuberance of its flamboyant decoration the structure remains simple; two superimposed octagons "pivoted" in relation to each other rest on pinnacles at each corner of the square tower. Each of these hold statues of three Apostles, which attend Christ, standing on the summit of the gable on the west face of the spire.

This is the highest stone spire in France, apart from that at Strasbourg. Jean de Beauce did not try to copy the neighbouring bell-tower : the great creative eras turned their back on mere imitation. He even gave to his work a different elevation, more in proportion to the nave, not forgetting that the Old Bell Tower was built to go with a church lower in height.

For this reason, it is the south parvis or square, near the **Rue aux Herbes** from which the **Old Tower** can be seen to better advantage; from that angle it emerges better from later buildings. The masses are masterfully organised, and the transition from the square tower to the spires' octagons is contrived with consummate art. From the ground the eye follows the vertical flight of the buttresses which is not interrupted by the pillars which frame the great openings at the base of the spire. A pyramid of angles and sharp gables join in the upward thrust of the great ribs, and this general interplay of obliques is subtly suggested long before the top of the square base is reached, in the subdued bevelling of the short columns placed at the re-entrant angles of the buttresses.

A few stone bell-towers are higher than the Old Tower — witness its neighbour — but the spire alone holds the record for overall height.

Its ribs pierce the sky in a jet of almost 164 feet; no superfluous ornament breaks its flow. It is hollow and does not rest on any framework; its walls diminish progressively from base to summit reducing from 32 to 12 inches. Each stone is cut in the form of a scale, which, projecting at the joint, prevents any penetration of rainwater. The Old Bell-tower, which has now been standing for eight centuries, was not shaken by the weight of bells, which collapsed onto the vault during the fire of 1194. Fire ravaged it again in 1836 and consumed the belfry. "Irreproachable spire", "King of Bell-Towers", it has been praised by both technicians and poets.

Viollet-le-Duc, often criticized, but who had acquired a deep knowledge of the buildings of the Middle Ages, was of the opinion that the old bell-tower of Chartres was the cleverest and sturdiest construction that he had ever encountered.

At the base of the tower, the **Angel of the Meridian,** a gracious statue-pillar of the same family as those of the great figures of the Royal Portal, holds towards the south her sundial (added in the 16th century). Both the angel and the sundial are copies, which were placed in position in 1974. The neighbouring abutment "Ass playing a hurdy-gurdy" illustrates a philosophical dictum of Boëthius.

SIDES OF THE NAVE.

Carried into effect before the Choir, the nave is strengthened by powerful flying buttresses, in the form of quarter-wheels; they in turn are braced by slender columns resembling spokes. To ensure solidity to this mass, each inclining column is monolithic, including both base and capital. The builder threw out right above the side aisles those stone crutches destined to counter the thrust of the high vaults and gave it an architectural effect which must have seemed daring. These are probably the oldest flying buttresses left to us from the Middle Ages. The upper part, added at an early date, rests on the bases provided for the pinnacles.

The projecting buttresses suggest cascading forces being fused. They retain an austerity still romanesque, and are only embellished by a row of figures in niches.

Inserted between two buttresses, the **Vendôme Chapel** was added, following a vow, by Count Louis de Bourbon-Vendôme, who, imprisoned, regained his freedom on Annunciation Day, 1413.

SOUTHERN FRONT.

As the old Western Façade was preserved, there was a pressing need to build a large front in the taste of the time. Instead of one, two were erected, the façades of the transept. Chartres is the only cathedral in which three façades of such importance are found, and where there are three groups of three doors; furthermore the six portals of the 13th century lie behind deep porches, and the sculptors took advantage of them to add a lavish wealth of sculpture.

The Southern Front is inspired by the great façade of Laon, then just built; and in its turn engendered that of Amiens.

Of the nine towers which should have graced the Cathedral, seven were unrealised : this is no disappointment. They all reached the level of the upper gallery; four towers of the lateral façades, two of the apse, and one which, invisible from the exterior, was started above the great central span.

The façades of the transept are sisters, but each has her individuality; on the southern one the buttresses are lightened by high and slender columns; the pillars of the porch are embellished with bas reliefs and a gallery of pinnacles runs between three stone gables.

THE CHEVET.

The **Chapel of Saint Piat** hugs the chevet, built as late as the 14th century, together with the Chapter-house on its ground floor. It communicates with the Cathedral by an elegant pierced staircase.

The **apse** opens its fan of flying buttresses above the trees of the garden. The choir, being surrounded by a double ambulatory, allows each of the flying buttresses two points of rest. The result is that their form is relieved, and yet it still remains similar to that of the nave.

The apsidal chapels are themselves supported by the chapels of the crypt. Among the latter the three most ancient (1020-1024) were encircled by a second wall in about 1200 and new narrower chapels have been inserted. Because of this the architect had to space the buttresses unevenly.

The weather-cock angel of the chevet was remade after the fire of 1836. The green colour of the copper roof harmonises happily with the Berchères stone.

Beyond the Sacristy, built at the end of the 13th century, and characterised by a huge window area, divided by mullions, one comes to the North Portal.

THE NORTH FRONT.

Started at the same time as the southern one, possibly a little earlier, the northern front was finished last. Here the procession of the great statues of the portals continues along the exterior pillars. The porch was planned from the beginning, and its foundations were laid at the same time as those of the portals. Deprived of the gallery which was to have crowned them, the gables remain austere. The towers, added while the work was in progress, lean, as do those of the south, against the pier prepared for the flying buttresses. Here the buttresses are graced by pedimented kiosks, following the plan adopted for the piers of the choir and chevet. Finally, sculptures jut out besides the Rose window.

At the foot of the New Bell Tower, Jean de Beauce built in the Renaissance style (1520) the Clock Pavilion, its face preserving its gilt and polychrome, which still tells the time.

A well can be seen at the foot of the first buttress of the nave, which has been built with a notch, to enable the buckets to be drawn up.

INTERNAL ARCHITECTURE.

It is by the Royal Portal that one should enter the Cathedral, at least for the first time. The size of the edifice, and the light which filters through the stained glass, stuns even the least informed visitors. Energy and power are combined to impress them. The masses fly up and fuse at the vaulting, but at the same time remain anchored to the ground. The rhythm of the piers, alternately cylindrical and octogonal, reminds one of the weak and strong supports of the first ogival churches with sexpartite vaults.

Forced to use as foundations the crypt of 1020, the architect of 1194 gave the nave the exceptional width of 54 feet (compared to Notre-Dame of Paris's 40 feet). The nave of Chartres is the widest nave of this type flanked by side aisles. Moreover the three doors of the front open into the central nave alone.

The architect, dependent on the 174-year old romanesque plan, conceived a quite new elevation, to be used later for the cathedrals of Soissons, Rheims and Amiens, amongst the most typical. Thanks to the flying buttresses, which balance the pressure of the high vaults, he does without tribunes, which, although beautiful, took up a third of the total height in earlier buildings, and thus interfered with its lighting. They were replaced by a triforium — which served as a gallery and promenoir.

Breaking away from Noyon, Paris, Laon, and also from Sens, it enabled him, for the first time, to give a greater height to the side aisles. Windows become much more important. In each bay of the highest floor even the twin lancets are surmounted by a Rose. Henceforth the problem of light was resolved, and from this experiment was born the form of gothic architecture in which fenestration predominates over wall area.

It is from the intersection of the transept and nave that one can compare the three great rose-windows, and the evolutions which took place while work was progressing. The Western Rose (1200 approximately) with a very successful and almost unique design includes large surfaces of wall between its medallions, of which each is of consequence. The Southern Rose, built about twenty years later, is composed of a network of slender mullions. Lastly the Northern Rose, commenced only a few years after, is a clerestory in which rose and lancets make up a whole.

The transept of Chartres is the most developed of such in France, apart from that of Laon (about 200 feet, nearly the length of Saint-Germain-des-Prés, in Paris). It includes the side aisles, a rare privilege, shared among others with Laon, Soissons, Rheims, Amiens, Rouen, Beauvais, York and Cologne. The architect had a free hand only with the foundations of the transept, but still had to reduce it in width in relations to the main nave. Furthermore certain irregularities appear, none in the least offensive, caused by having to adjust it to the rest of the original ground plan.

At the intersection of the transept, the cluster of columns shoot up in one jet as far as the spring of the arches. They are a replica of those at the far end of the nave, raised against the angles of the romanesque towers.

The choir, the largest in France, has a double ambulatory. This has taken on a new look since the construction of the cloister of the choir in the 16th century. The play of piers and vaults — still irregular there, but always logical — together with the coloured effects caused by the stained glass, set on varied planes, gives this part of the cathedral an individuality which can never be forgotten.

THE ROYAL PORTAL.

Still romanesque in its ornamental richness, the Royal Portal, sculpted about 1145-50, already augurs the Gothic portals by the presence of its great statues. It is one of the best preserved of this transitional period; certainly the most important apart from that of Saint-Denis, in Paris, which unfortunately has been badly disfigured.

The Lord in Majesty with the features of Christ sits enthroned in the central tympanum, while two angels at the top of the arch bring the royal crown, the subjects of this portal describe the "Kingdom of God" temporally and spatially; the statuette on the left, above Eve, is probably Abraham between his two wives, who gave him his descendants, and this retinue ends with the remotest peoples of the earth suggested on the extreme right by an asiatic king. This statue and the neighbouring one, struck by the disease of stone were taken down and put away at the beginning of 1975. Since 1974 three statue-columns and a small column have been replaced by copies. Five out of twenty-four of the statues have disappeared in the past.

Its vertical rhythm, underlined by the elongated forms and immobility of the great statues, gives this illustrious line a nobility which has no equivalent elsewhere. Difficult to identify with any certainty — several of them are more than likely the kings of Juda — they all show in their faces an intense inner life. A slight smile can even be discerned, known as the "Smile of Chartres". The statues of the central door are the work of a master. Notice the scintillating glance of the queen on the right (the Queen of Sheba). The female costumes give evidence of the French styles of the 12th century.

The geometrical decoration of the columns are varied, and the subjects of the small columns have an exuberant fantasy. The statuettes are ranged in sixes over the frames of the door and among the angels are interspersed men of all types, prophets, kings, scholars, even a trouvere, a butcher, and a robber.

In the capitals the Flight into Egypt, the Massacre of the Innocents, the Last Supper, the Kiss of Judas, are amongst the easier ones to decipher. In the lintel of the right-hand door are depicted scenes from the birth of the Messiah, of which there is a racy Message to the Shepherds; the pan-pipe player is gaping at hearing the great news. In the tympanum, the Virgin Mother presents the Infant Jesus — a statue later copied at St. Anne's portal of Notre-Dame of Paris. "Seat of Widsom", she is not only surrounded by angels, but also by the sages of antiquity, and allegories of the liberal arts. Thus one sees amongst others Aristotle with a desk on his knees, his brow furrowed by throught, above whom stands the image of Dialectic; then Cicero and Rhetoric; Astronomy gazing at the sky and Ptolemy; a diverting Grammar with her cane ready to punish lazy scholars, and finally Music with Pythagoras, the great therorist of Rhythm. The presence of the Gemini and the Pisces makes us return to the composition on the left, where the Ascension is framed by the curves of the Calendar. Signs of the Zodiac alternate with the occupations of the months; one notes amongst others Capricorn, a well-conceived imaginary being, and Scorpio with a human face, two-headed Janus dividing the Twelfth-Cake, April clasping a flourishing tree, the departure of a falcon hunt, Harvest-time. Threshing, Vintage, and a peasant killing his pig. Thus opposing, and complementary to each other, are found occupations of a material and spiritual nature.

It all brings us back to the central composition, inspired by the Apocalypse of Saint John. By 1145, Christ and the Four Animals was already an ancient theme. But here the three-dimensional sculpture asserts itself and serenity replaces the somewhat wild character of the earlier tympanums. The sculptor chose a somewhat banal human model for his "Christ", and then breathed a supernatural majesty into it. The Apostles line up on the lintel and in the arch near the angels; the twenty-four ancients hold their musical instruments, faithfully reproducing those then in use.

The Royal Portal had a leading influence on art, far beyond the frontiers of France.

THE NORTHERN PORTAL.

CENTRE : The whole sculptural design of the northern front is concerned with the Union of God and Man. Some time elapsed between the earliest statues of the Portal proper and the sculptures of the Porch. Here is a quite noticeable evolution in style. The exterior central arches are full of fine sculptures describing the Creation and the Fall of Man. Eve is spinning and Adam digging — and God blesses their work. In the central doorway itself are seen the statues of Old Testament characters who prophesied the Coming of Christ, ranged in chronological sequence. They surround Saint Anne who, on a pier, presents the infant Mary. Here are Melchizedek, Abraham about to sacrifice Isaac, Moses pointing to Airain snake, Aaron, rather than Samuel, David, then Isaiah above the sleeping Jesse, Jeremiah, Simeon, Saint John the Baptist, unequalled masterpieces of 13th century statuary, and Saint Peter who, standing parallel to Melchizedek, emphasises the continuity between the Old and the New Law. At the feet of Jeremiah, man listens, at the feet of Simeon he understands the word of God. On the outermost piers of the central Porch, high-reliefs and great statues refer, on the right, to the History of Samuel and the Ark of the Covenant, on the left to that of David; there one can see an astonishing interpretation of Goliath as a roman officer, and an expressive statue of a woman in 13th century costume in which one can discern Bethsheba.

In the arches of the portal the Line of David appears amongst branches, symbolic of the Tree of Jesse, near the patriarchs and prophets. All contemplate the masterful scenes on the lintel and tympanum of the Dormition, the Assumption, and the Crowning of the Virgin.

RIGHT-HAND SIDE

The right-hand doorway illustrates the idea of human wisdom, as derived from Divine Wisdom, in various degrees. In the group of Balaam on his she-ass, in the figures of the Queen of Sheba and Solomon, a happy naturalism breaks through; the young pagan queen is positioned obliquely and seems to be moving towards the wise king whose body turns majestically to welcome her. The fool Marcoulf is, in antithesis, sculpted in the pediment. Beneath the queen a black slave with his bowl and purse full of money, is strikingly lifelike. The door jamb on the right is filled by Jesus Ben Sira, author of Ecclesiastes, and the re-building of the temple of Jerusalem, then Judith standing on a dog as a symbol of her fidelity, finally Joseph bearing the attributes of his power in Egypt. On the plinth, the temptation of Putiphar's wife is treated with a consummate mastery of movement.

The Judgement of Solomon, on the lintel, and Job, on the tympanum, are accompanied, in the arch, by the stories of Samson and Gideon, Esther, Judith, and Tobias. The exterior arches show a series of the **Zodiac,** which follows in parallel that of the **Months.** May giving water to her falcon is a charming statuette, so is Winter turning his bare foot towards the fire, and Summer walking briskly and hardly clothed with his arms full of leaves. Beneath the great statues of the porch, human activities are described; stock-farming and tilling, music and industry on the left, while opposite one notices near the Doctor, the Architect with his right-angle rule, the Painter with his palette, the Philosopher and the Alchemist, and amongst much vegetable decoration, inspired by garden plants, wild paths or forest trees, one can see an interpretation of a raspberry cane, very lifelike and "appliqued" on the column which it adorns.

At the angle of the porch, next to Saint Savinien, is Saint Modeste, a most graceful female figure by an anonymous sculptor who also worked on the portal of the clock-tower of Strasbourg cathedral.

LEFT-HAND SIDE

In the Annunciation and the Visitation, the pedestals seem to pivot and the statues seem to converse. Noticeable also are mutilations which took place during the Revolution, but luckily Sergent, of the Convention, soon put a stop to this. The head of the Angel Gabriel which had been given anonymously to a Learned Society in 1863, was recovered and identified, and in 1959 put back in place.

The Wisdom of the christian era is illustrated in the tympanum by the Shepherds and the Magi, while the Virtues, the Wise Virgins contrasted with the Foolish Virgins, decorate the arches. Outside, delicate statuettes represent the Joys of the Spirit and Body, adjacent to the contrasting figures of active and meditative life. The latter prays while the former, a truly documentary piece, devotes his time to working wool, flax and hemp.

The northern portal, influenced by Senlis, in its turn influenced

PORTAIL SUD 40. LE CHRIST ENSEIGNANT
41. ENSEMBLE

40

PORCHE SUD

42. PERSONNAGES DE L'ANCIEN TESTAMENT
43. DÉTAIL DU TRUMEAU
44. PILIER DES MARTYRS
    MORT DE SAINT THOMAS BECKET
45. CORTÈGE DES DAMNÉS

43

42

46-47. GRANDE ROSE ET VERRIÈRES DE LA FAÇADE OCCIDENTALE

48. NOTRE-DAME DE LA BELLE VERRIÈRE
49. LANCETTES DE LA FAÇADE SEPTENTRIONALE : SAINTE ANNE ET SALOMON
50. VITRAIL DE CHARLEMAGNE. JOUTE DE ROLAND ET DE FERRAGUT

49

51

54

52

53

VITRAIL DU CALENDRIER

51. LE SAGITTAIRE
52. LA BALANCE
53. DÉCEMBRE. L'ABATTAGE
    DU PORC
54. LE CHRIST

55. VERRIÈRES DE L'ÉGLISE
    SAINT-PIERRE

56. NOTRE-DAME DU PILIER

Amiens, Strasbourg and Lausanne; and at least one of its sculptors worked at Rheims.

THE SOUTHERN PORTAL.

The southern portal is that of the "Grace of the New Covenant". The pinnacled gallery of the porch shelters the Messiah's forebears; the first on the left is David. Christ rests against the pier of the middle door, above Charity, teaching the Apostles who are lined up on either side; Saint Peter can be seen on the left, while Saint Paul, Saint John, and Saint James the Greater stand on the right.

The tympanum and arch describe the Resurrection of the Dead, and the Last Judgement, at which the nine choirs of angels are present. Surrounded by the Instruments of the Passion, Our Saviour displays his wounds; Mary and Saint John plead for Mankind. The lintel shows Saint Michael weighing souls. The procession of the Chosen, in which all social states are suggested, stretches towards the left, while into the Mouth of Hell, on the right, are hurled the Damned. Here a king and a bishop can be seen, as well as amongst the Blessed. At the extreme right, grinning devils drag down the Miser and the Courtesan. The last subject on the side of Paradise is a king exchanging his crown for the crown of the Elect.

The musicians of the Apocalypse rise in tiers on two sides of the external pillars. Virtues and Vices alternate on the other faces of these pillars; the Virtues are sitting on thrones, each of them holding an emblazoned coat of arms while the Vices are in full activity. Despair is a woman stabbing herself with a sword, Greed is counting the wealth of his coffers, Pride is thrown from the horse on which he was parading, Hardheartedness thanking her benefactor by a kick in the stomach, Cowardice fleeing from a hare, leaving his arms behind, Inconstancy is shown as a monk leaving his habit at the abbey door and, still tonsured, escaping in his shirt; lastly, to illustrate Discord, is a married couple fighting and upsetting a pitcher while the distaff remains idle. All these scenes, in high relief, recapture in an even more lively way, the subjects of the bas-reliefs which had just been sculpted on the lower part of the main portal of Notre-Dame of Paris.

Martyrs and Confessors share the lateral portals. On the lintel and tympanum on the left, as well as on the lower vaulting, is illustrated the stoning of Saint Stephen. In the place of honour is Christ, wearing a royal crown and holding the Palm of Martyrdom. In the arch are the Innocents, then a multitude of martyrs who collect the blood of the Lamb. Opposite the group of statues of Saint Stephen, — a close relative of that at Sens — Saint Clement and Saint Laurence, stand three statues stamped by archaism, one of which is St. Vincent.

They contrast with the two statues added in front which are finely finished. The one on the left standing opposite Saint George, whose identity is a subject of controversy remains an unforgettable figure of knighthood. It is probably Roland.

At the Door of the Confessors the group on the right is one of the masterpieces of mediaeval statuary; in these effigies of Saint Martin, the leader, Saint Jerome the intellectual, and the pope, Saint Gregory, their individual personalities are strongly expressed.

The Biblical texts translated by St. Jerome is a parchment scroll unrolled as far as the plinth, where the Synagogue, blindfolded, consults it, but it remains incomprehensible to her. St. Nicholas, St. Ambrose and St. Sylvester fill the embrasures on the left, together with St. Laurence whose posture and draping show a slightly later period. This is also the case with St. Avit, which makes a pair. Above the door, stories of St. Martin and St. Nicolas are illustrated, while lower down in the arch other saints in ranks are set in tiers; the horizontal part describes the legend of St. Giles.

Besides these, forty-eight episodes from the lives of saints are sculpted on the corner-pillars of the porch. Amongst those on the pillar of the martyrs one can recognize the decapitation of St. John the Baptist,as well as St. Eustace and his family within the blazing bull, St. Laurence on the grill, the body of St. Vincent thrown up on the shore and protected by wild beasts, St. Blaise skinned alive and — a fact which was then a recent event — St. Thomas à Becket murdered in Canterbury Cathedral. On the Confessors' pillar are depicted, among others, the christening of Clovis by St. Remy and St. Anthony tempted by the devil during his meditations.

The value of the sculptures of Chartres is in their authenticity as well as in their inspiration and style.

STAINED GLASS.

In their quality and quantity the stained glass windows of the Cathedral form a collection unique in the world. Their area alone is considerably over 2.400 square yards.

The **three western windows,** glazed about 1150, had given light to the earlier cathedral. They were preserved from the fire of 1194 by the tribune of the narthex, the level of which can be gauged by the base of the columns placed between the windows.

Their colours range from the pure blue of the Tree of Jesse to the gold of the stained glass of the Passion and Resurrection, the transition being secured by the tones which illuminate the central panel.

The contrast remains no matter what variations of light occur due to the time of day or the season. The direct light kindles the reds and yellows; in shadow the blues are magnified.

The genealogy of Christ illustrated by the Tree of Jesse is a theme which Suger had created a few years earlier at Saint Denis. It is conceded that the perfection of this window at Chartres has not been attained by any other. The great window of the Childhood of Christ, reaching higher than three floors (about 36 feet — each panel alone measures more than 3 feet) is formed in checkers; round scenes on blue backgrounds alternate with square scenes on red backgrounds. At the apex, the Virgin in Majesty was inspired by the byzantine tradition.

Notre-Dame of the "Belle Verrière" (the second window of the south ambulatory) also dates from the 12th century. Its luminous blues stand out from deep reds. The remaining glass, later than 1200, serves as a framework.

All the other glass, with a very few exceptions, was made during the first third of the 13th century. Those nearer the ground are ornamented, some of them by ironwork of varying designs. Large scale figures fill the upper windows.

The "blue of Chartres" has acquired notoriety. In fact the blues, no more than other tones, are not perceptibly different from those found elsewhere which are of the same age. Those of Bourges for instance were fashioned by the same hands. But the stained glass shows up best if spared garish light, and light at Chartres cathedral alone, or perhaps also at Sainte Chapelle in Paris, fulfil these conditions. Glass, stained in the mass, retains its strength of colour after centuries. The lead in which they are inserted stresses the outlines. Only certain flesh tints have darkened. The exterior of the glass — between two and six mms. thick — has been attacked by atmospheric agents, which further increases the refraction, already obtained originally by deliberate mistakes. The richest glass is that which during its blowing has been ribbed or buckled, or blistered by bubbles.

Set in place while the building was going on, the stained glass follows a predetermined plan, in the main axes and chapels; a certain fantasy prevails elsewhere, leaving room for the illustration of popular legends.

The north front, the darker side — only catching the last rays of a summer evening — depicts the Old Testament awaiting the Messiah. The axial lancets of the choir, which light up in the morning, show the coming of the " Light of the World ". The Last Judgement faces the setting sun, which evokes the End of the World.

The Southern Rose, where the light reaches maximum brilliance, is consecrated to the Glory of Christ. Below, the artist represents with audacious mastery the four great prophets carrying on their shoulders the four evangelists, thus expressing the bonds between the Old and

New Law. The Coat of Arms of Dreux-Bretagne reminds one of the donor, Pierre Mauclerc.

The northern group, including the Rose of France, was paid for, towards the completion of the work, by Blanche of Castille and the King; the Lys of France and the Castle of Spain can be seen there. It is possible that the features of Solomon (2nd lancet from the right) were inspired by those of Louis IX then still a young man.

As in the corresponding portal, the main figure is that of St. Anne, and Melchizedek, David and Aaron are again seen. The lower panels describe the idolatry of Nebuchadnezzar, Saul's despair, the madness of Jeroboam who set up the Golden Calf, and the fury of Pharaoh confounded in his pursuit of the Hebrews.

All the stained glass is by anonymous artists, yet the only glass-marker of that time known to us is Clement of Chartres, who signed a window at Rouen. Many of the windows carry figurative signatures of associations of artisans and shopkeepers who donated them : bakers, cobblers, grocers, haberdashers, apothecaries, stonemasons, butchers, coopers, carpenters and cartwrights, tavernkeepers even; we can see at work, at the bottom of the Redemption window, blacksmiths; and in the window of St. James, a furrier showing a squirrel coat to a lady who is feeling it with her bare hand.

The window of the Assumption is a short documentary of the art of cobbling; there an armourer hammers a spur, there a weaver handles his loom, elsewhere money-changers examine coins or value jewelry. Carpenters set their saws exactly as they do today; the shoe-seller, exhibits his wares laced up at the ankles as was fashionable then, cathedral-builders mount ladders, a trough of mortar on their shoulders, while a sculptor rests by his roughhewn stone to quench his thirst. In a little rose-window the ploughmen of Nogent — the inscription does not designate which Nogent — are depicted with their plough and yoke. This is the fullest account which has reached us of popular life during the reign of Philippe Auguste.

Other donors were princes and kings, knights and ecclesiastics and pilgrims, indeed some of them were on their way to St. James of Compostella. The people of Tours gave three windows and those of Poitiers probably did likewise.

Amongst this mass of stained glass of outstanding importance in the history of art, how can one pick out specific subjects ? In the south aisle of the nave the story of St. John the Evangelist consists of deep blues and dull browns, the simple scenes depicting St. Mary Magdelene have a rich mosaïc background of blue scales; the neighbouring window shows the parable of the Good Samaritan and beside there is the story of Adam and Eve, establishing an analogy between succouring the infirm and the atonement of mankind. In the window of the Assumption, one notices the wonderful Dormition of the Virgin, the setting of which no doubt inspired the sculptor of a tympanum at Strasbourg. The building site of Chartres and its pilgrims are brought alive in the window of the Miracles.

In the northern side aisle is seen the story of Noah and the Flood, the life of St. Lubin told in vigorous style, the legend of St. Eustace which reads like a novel, transcribed by a clever glass blower, a lover of delicate shades and elegant design; then the thrilling tale of Joseph and the caravan of old Jacob travelling towards Egypt, the life of St. Nicholas with its popular ring, adjacent to the window of the Redemption with its clever parallels.

Past the angle of the north transept is the parable of the Infant Prodigy together with all that the artist has added to the evangelical text. In the ambulatory and the chapels one stops more readily before the romance of St. Julian the Hospitaler, or the celebrated window of Charlemagne which portrays one of the oldest illustrations of the Song of Roland; or in front of the window of St. James, its neighbour, equally rich in tones, or the symphony of blue of St. Sylvester's window, or the reds of St. Stephen windows. There are the martyrs' windows, then those of the Apostles and further along those of the Confessors. This one relates the life of St. Thomas à Becket, another the miracles of St. Martin. Near the story of the Holy Virgin is the window of the Calendar in which are juxtaposed the labours of the months with the signs of the Zodiac.

Of the first floor windows, one must mention, apart from the groups in the apse and three façades, the window of Jean Clement of Mez who accepts the oriflamme of St. Denis, in the south transept; in the nave, the large figure of St. George as a knight, to the north, and to the south St. James, recognisable by his shells. Also notice the small rose window of the Virgin of Wisdom which occupies the north wall of the nave.

In the roses of the choir windows, great lords are riding. Louis of France, eldest son of Philippe Auguste, Thibault count of Chartres, Simon de Montfort, his son Amaury possibly, and many others; for example the king of Castile, kinsman to the Queen of France, who is accompanied by a white greyhound, while mounted on an almost black horse, which stands out against a deep blue background, where waves his red banner on which is shown a gold castle.

Since the end of the 13th century and in the 14th century, rich grisailles replaced several stained glass windows. The Vendome chapel was glazed during the 15th century.

One window of the south transept, deprived of its stained glass since 1791, received some new in 1954 carried out by F. Lorin, a great artist in stained-glass from Chartres; paid for by Architects of the United States, it relates the life of Saint Fulbert. On the northern arm of the transept, the window of biblical symbols by the same artist was a gift from the Germans in 1971. Thus in the same building, one can follow the evolution of glazing through the ages.

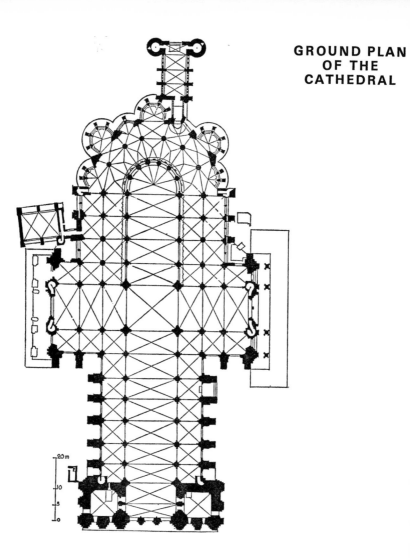

20 m

10

5

0

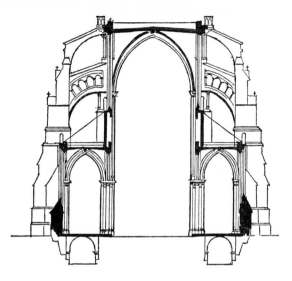

SECTION
AND
ELEVATION
OF THE
CATHEDRAL

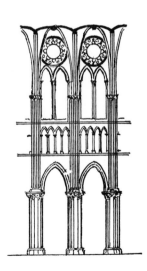

THE ENCLOSURE OF THE CHOIR.

Commenced by Jean de Beauce in 1514 in the flamboyant style, and completed during the Renaissance fifteen years later, the enclosure of the choir stuns by the prodigality of its sculptures. The design of the great scenes from the life of the Virgin and Christ was decided by canon Mainterne, but the work was carried out in various stages. The first segment, to the south, was sculpted by Jean Soulas under Francis 1st. They are among the most arresting, particularly the announcement to St. Anne of her impending maternity, her encounter with Joachim before the golden gate of Jerusalem, and the birth of Mary, with the preparation for the first bath. Their elegance is tempered by a domesticity suggested by contemporary costumes and furniture.

Slightly earlier, a sculptor, whose name is unknown to us, had started the last scenes, to the north, as far as the "Crowning of Our Lady". Their compact composition contains also some archaisms of style, but their spiritual content is possibly more apparent than those of the rest of the enclosure.

Between the 16th and 18th centuries, various artists worked on the other groups. Jean Soulas probably sculpted the first twelve groups to the south, including the Adoration of the Magi, with its smiling Virgin and its mischievous Infant Jesus. François Marchand succeeded him. Amongst other works, he was responsible for the Massacre of the Innocents, and the bas-relief of the Flight into Egypt, placed next to each other. In 1611 the work of Thomas Boudin shows up better in the incredulity of St. Thomas, or the Holy Women at the Tomb, than in other scenes signed by him, such as the Transfiguration in which the influence of Michelangelo is still obvious. During Louis XIV's reign, Jean de Dieu and Pierre Legros were working, the former on the scene of the woman taken in adultery, the latter on the Healing of the man born blind; both works show great warmth of feeling. Tuby, whose father sculpted groups in the park of Versailles, worked on the episode of the Palms. Lastly, an important sequence of subjects were entrusted to Simon Mazières, of which the Flagellation and a dramatic Crucifixion are particularly noteworthy.

The forty scenes cover a distance of 270 feet. The enclosure of the choir is mostly built of soft stone from Tonnerre. Even if their appearance amongst 13th century architecture seems out of place to the purist it must be admitted that it surpasses in size and splendour any comparable work.

The fine chiselling of the buttresses and stylobates shows an inexhaustable verve when embellishing the theme of profane fauns, cupids, cornucopias, Dolphins and other figures of trophies. Note the prodigious audacity of the flamboyant pinnacles at the end bays,

59

**60. CLOTURE
DU CHŒUR.
L'ADORATION
DES MAGES**

61. DALLAGE DE LA NEF.
    CENTRE DU LABYRINTHE

    ANCIEN JUBÉ
62. LA NATIVITÉ
63. LE SOMMEIL DES MAGES

64

66

64. DÉTAIL DU BAS-RELIEF FIGURANT LE MONDE TERRESTRE
65. ANIMAUX ET DÉCOR VÉGÉTAL
66. CHASSEUR

67. LA SALLE A L'ITALIENNE
68-69. CROIX PROCESSION-
NELLE ET CROSSE EN
ÉMAIL CHAMPLEVÉ

68

69

the most important of which are actual miniature clock-towers.

The medallions of the stylobates, in the round part, illustrate some Old Testament episodes, and legends of ancient mythology. The first one to the south recalls the raising of the siege of Chartres by Rollon. Other medallions to the north frame profiles of Roman emperors.

During the rebuilding of the choir, in the 18th century, the enclosure was mutilated, both north and south, by being broken up by large marble framed doorways; and in 1792 the astronomical clock was deprived of its mechanism, which was melted down for ammunition.

To the left of the clock face, strange bas-reliefs stand out from a slightly curved background which surrounds the well of a minute spiral staircase by which the clock might be reached for winding. The stair is lit by a small window still retaining its wrought iron. The most interesting of the remaining carved wood doors is that which opens onto the group showing the Presentation of Mary at the temple.

OTHER SCULPTURES, PAVING, ORGANS.

At the end of Louis XV's reign, Bridan was invited to sculpt the monumental Assumption of the High Altar and the six bas-reliefs of white marble which cut off the enclosure.

The 20th century discreetly added to the side aisles the Stations of the Cross by Saupique. Eight hundred years have passed since the Capitals at the entrance of the lower room of the northern bell tower were chiselled, depicting scenes of violence, and which are the oldest sculptures in the Cathedral.

The paving of the Nave and its side aisles, set on a slight incline, allowed the floor to be swilled out more easily after pilgrims had been camping in the church. Until a century ago, to the north side by the clock, could be seen a cistern receiving rain water for that purpose. There still remains a channel worn in the wall by the second bay. Towards the middle of the nave, the Labyrinth, or Road to Jerusalem is in its original state, as is the rest of the paving; a road of symbolic pilgrimage, its winding path is almost one thousand feet in length.

The great organ case, with its lantern turrets, dates from 1542, and rests on a balcony of the 14th century.

If Chartres cathedral is conspicuous by its lack of tombs, this is due to symbolic tradition. It is placed under the protection of our Lady of the Assumption, and Christendom, as we know, has always assumed that the concomitants of death were spared to the Virgin.

OUR LADY OF THE PILLAR.
ROOD SCREEN. TREASURY.
THE VIRGIN'S VEIL.

The statue of "Our Lady of the Pillar" dressed in sumptuous clothes, is always surrounded by a blazing mass of candles. Carved about 1507 in pear-wood, she has retained in parts her polychrome painting. At first she was called the "Black Virgin" to distinguish her from another statue, this one made of alabaster. She was set up in front of the choir near the central arcade of the rood screen. At the time when this latter was destroyed she was placed against a pillar of the transept crossing; removed in 1791, she was forgotten and it was this that saved her from the revolutionaries. Since 1806 she has been resting on a column of the old rood screen, hence she was given her new name. The pseudo-gothic woodwork dates from between 1831-1836.

The treasure of the Cathedral, dispersed by the Revolution, has recovered some of its valuable pieces. It is set out in the Saint-Piat Chapel in the chevet, which can be reached by a stairway leading up from the cloister.

Above the central window, the veil of Our Lady, a gift from Charles the Bald (see page 13) is displayed in a monstrance which dates from the last century. The shrine made by Teudon at the end of the 10th century was opened for the first time in 1712. It disclosed that the relic was a veil and not a chemise, as had been believed for a long time, hence the medal in the form of a small chemise which the pilgrim to Chartres wore.

Whenever the Queens of France were pregnant they were given by the Chapter a chemise which had touched the reliquary of the "Sainte chemise" of Our Lady.

On certain Sundays and holidays, the veil is displayed in the cathedral itself on the altar of "Our Lady of the Pillar".

Amongst the objects of the treasury, properly so-called, you will observe the great chest of the 13th century, forming a triptych and decorated with raised enamels from Limoges which are set out in the centre; and in the same case a 16th reliquary containing a gold and ivory cross from the 11th century, a 13th century crozier, an incense boat from the end of the Middle-Ages, various pieces of jewellery and holy vessels, among them a chalice offered by Henri III; two golden hearts donated ex voto by Louis XVI and his Sister, lady Elisabeth.

Other offerings made ex voto can be seen laid out in the chapel : the 14th century royal helmet, which probably belonged to Charles VI, a coat of mail which is perhaps the one worn by Philippe le Bel at the Battle of Mons-en-Puelle (1304) and a child's coat of mail; finally two belts sent by some tribes of American Indians in the 17th century.

The other cases are filled up with precious materials, like the Veil of the Empress Irene (8th century), the sumptuous cloak donated in the 17th century for the "Black Virgin" and the small damask garment (16th century) which suited the old statue of "Notre-Dame de Sous Terre". Certain richly embroidered liturgical adornments are thought to be a gift from Anne of Austria.

Attention should also be drawn to the chasuble, the embroidery of which was done for Henry IV's coronation. The huge lectern in the form of an eagle was not so long ago still in the choir of the cathedral.

The rood screen was built in the reign of Saint Louis. The gallery was supported by columns; it consisted of seven arched bays set out towards the nave with arcades topped by gables. It was destroyed in 1763 in a savage manner. Its sculptures most of which were mutilated were buried on the spot and have since been rediscovered. They are on display with the treasure in the Saint-Piat Chapel. Certain of them are classed among the most admirable works of art of the 13th century. The Nativity amongst others, with the obviously maternal posture of the Virgin and the solicitous gestures of St Joseph is a model of composition and execution. The same goes for the Sleep of the Magi, lying side by side, their feet against the stable wall, from which horses can be seen emerging, already harnessed for the journey. Originality and freshness of thought express themselves in realism, well suited to the decorative frame that it adorns. In addition to the Message to the Shepherds and the Presentation at the temple, let us also mention certain keystones, that of Christ and the four Evangelists, that of the Virgin surrounded by angels and that of the Annunciation with its frieze of wild roses. At the side of the columns bearing the capitals of the rood screen, you will note finally a large bas-relief with animal figures and hunting scenes. Above the door has been placed a statue of Christ (13th century) which used to top the west gable (replaced by a copy since 1853).

The Saint-Piat Chapel, an elegant 14th century construction, is decorated for the most part with stained glass windows of the same period. The great window of the chevet, with its last judgement and figures of saints is interesting because of its architectural decorations, alternately inspired by religious building and military constructions. The stained glass window near to the north entrance dates from the 16th century; here you can see the Virgin with the Baby Jesus and the donor kneeling before them.

CRYPT AND TOWERS.

The crypt of Saint Fulbert (1020-1024) shelters the sanctuary of "Notre-Dame-Sous-Terre" and the **Well of the Saint-Forts,** down which, according to tradition, were precipitated the Martyrs of Chartres.

The three principal chapels, also of the 11th century, radiate out, and are cradle-vaulted; four others, added in about 1200, are characterised by their rudimentary ogival vaults and by their larger windows.

The cathedral font located in the southern gallery of the crypt, is a square monolithic baptismal basin of the 12th century with a column at each corner.

By ascending the towers one can understand better the structure of the building, particularly the flying buttresses. Observe the burnt corner of the New Bell-Tower by the nave roof. From the adjoining bay from which one gets a plunging view on to the romanesque tower, notice the eight inner abutments thrown up by Jean de Beauce to sustain the weight of the spire. To the spiral staircase built on the same clever principle as those of the 12th or 13th centuries, is added an improvement. The moulded stair rail is cut into the central support. One of its windows enables one to catch sight, while passing, of the huge Great Bell weighing about six tons; the New-Bell Tower contains seven bells, the total weight of which is approximately nineteen tons.

From the square flat roof, placed on a level with the great statues of the Apostles, many details of the old Bell Towers, not obvious from the ground, can be appreciated. The public is allowed as far as this floor, 220 feet high (324 steps up, of which 194 only reach the roof gallery) from which they can view a wide horizon. The axis of the main roof is directed towards Paris. At the same time a general view of the town can be enjoyed, with its network of narrow streets and picturesque old roofs.

THE TOWN

THE CLOISTER AREA
AND 13th CENTURY HOUSES.

The Cloister of Our Lady, or the Cathedral canons' quarter, was entered by nine doors. Two of them remain, of which one is in the Rue Saint-Yves, facing the North Porch. The hinge-pin of the door and its chains can still be seen. The houses of the North Cloister form a group full of character. Opposite the Royal Portal stands a 13th century house. It has wonderful windows with sculpted tympanums : foliated arabesques, winged griffons, and also an amusing wrestling scene, coming straight from the notebooks of Villard de Honnecourt.

Another 13 th century house, but restored (at the angle of the Rue des Changes, to the South) shows tympanums with "Têtes de feuilles". From a third (No. 6) a grotesque mask projects on the left hand side, above the ground floor.

On the Cathedral square, near the Syndicat d'Initiative (Touring Office) and giving access to the Chamber of Commerce garden, is a railing of bronze and wrought-iron, finished in 1769. In the Cathedral it replaced the rood screen which had just been destroyed.

THE FORMER EPISCOPAL PALACE
AND ITS GARDENS. THE MUSEUM.

Another 18th century entrance gate near the Cathedral porch leads one into the Garden of Honour of the episcopal Palace, the front of which is a fine example of Louis XIII architecture, of pink brick consolidated by white stone chiselled with vermiculated or geometric motives. This was built by Bishop Leonor d'Estampes de Valançay. Nevertheless it was Mgr. de Fleury, who caused the Entrance Pavilion to be erected, in 1748 or so, and in 1760 the section on the extreme left was built.

Beyond the arcades (latter part of 16th century), the only remains of the outhouses, the terrace allows a fine view of the lower town and the Church of Saint-André. On this side, a lawn preceeds the wing added in 1705 by Mgr. de Godet des Marais, a councillor to Mme de Maintenon.

From the narrow terrace which juts out into the Old Orangery, other views can be obtained over the valley. One can see at the far end of the garden, beyond the Chevet of the Saint-Piat Chapel, the gothic nave of Saint Pierre.

The former Bishop's Palace shelters the **Municipal Museum**, one of the most interesting of provincial museums. To the diversity and excellence of the objects displayed is added the quality of its architectural setting. The drawing rooms, filled with period furniture, give the visitor the impression that they are still lived in.

In the Vestibule of Honour, is a double ramp of wrought-iron by de Gamain, whose son was to teach Louis XVI the art of locksmithing. The room in the Italian manner, to the left, was designed by the architect Godot, as was the vestibule. Louis XV ironwork runs the length of the gallery. On the wall panels are sculpted roses, the flowery coat of arms of Mgr. de Fleury. Two works only are shown here, a 14th century wayside cross, of which the central quatrefoil, facing both ways, displays the stigmata and death of Saint Francis of Assisi ; and Saint Paul, by François Marchand (16th century) obviously inspired by Michelangelo's Moses. It is in this room where each summer are given the chamber concerts known as the "Samedis musicaux de Chartres".

The **Chapel**, by Rousset, can be compared with the better religious buildings of the 18th century. The altar and its decoration remain intact, as does the coloured marble parquetry floor in which Fleury's roses again appear. In the Assumption, by Bridan, the Virgin is a cast, the original having been placed in the Church of Saint Pierre. In the Chapel are shown enamels of the **twelve Apostles,** produced for Francis 1st by Leonard Limosin. The freshness of their colours and their large surface made their firing a **tour de force** and class them amongst the most outstanding of such works.

The windows of the passage to the side of the Chapel open on to a small interior courtyard, which the oldest part of the bishop's palace, retains its mediaeval aspect.

The location of the various displays may vary, depending on the exhibitions being held; only the principal show pieces are mentioned here. Amongst precious old objects, various inlaid enamels can be seen : a gable of a reliquary, a processional cross, a crozier, pyxis and other rare pieces; an ivory Tau Cross of the 12th century, a bronze measure dated 1283, an embroidered triptych of the 15th century and several illuminated manuscripts.

Of the sculptures, apart from the two already mentioned, the 12th century Christ in Majesty, a Saint John the Evangelist of the 13th century, and a Virgin and Child of the 15th, should not be overlooked.

Paintings of the principal schools are represented. Notice particularly the " Virgin surrounded by Saints " from the studio of Fra Angelico, some Flemish, German and Italian primitives, a Saint Lucy by Zurbaran, and several Fragonards. The collection of portraits is especially rich, with an Erasmus by Holbein, Molière painted by Mignard, Turenne by Philippe de Champaigne, Fontenelle by Largillière, the Duc de Saint-Simon when a child, by Rigaud. Other artists whose paintings are exhibited include Quentin Metzys, Coypel, Lesueur, Deruet, Ribera, Chardin, Van Loo, Nanteuil, Boucher, Mme Vigée-Lebrun, Teniers, Hubert Robert, Greuze, Prud'hon and Puvis de Chavannes; without listing the watercolour artists, painters of gouaches, miniatures and pastels. Among the latter is a lively portrait by Ducreux.

The museum exhibits several collections of tapestries : the Moses series (Bruxelles, 16th century) the Hunt of Maximilian (Gobelins) and the Loves of the Gods, after Boucher. This latter embellishes the great Salon reserved for the 18th century. Here terrestrial and celestial spheres can be seen, belonging to the Marquise de Pompadour, from the château she owned in the village of Crecy, near Chartres. Other rooms on the ground floor are dedicated to the local art of the district, which once flourished; souvenirs of Marceau, and works of the engraver Sergent, his brother-in-law; lastly those reserved for antiquities and Far Eastern art.

On the first floor are found the works of contemporary painters; also engravings, pottery and ceramics, arms and armour, folk art and anything concerning the history of the cathedral.

Also nearby one should visit the Cellar of Loëns and the old Town market (rue du Cardinal-Pie), which enjoys a picturesque site on the way to Rue Saint-Yves and the Cathedral.

THE CELLAR OF LOËNS.

At 5, Rue du Cardinal-Pie (almost opposite the Rue de l'Horloge) the Chapter's building, where the tithes were stored, was traditionally named Loëns. This word is Danish in origin, and means "a barn", and was no doubt introduced during the 9th century invasions.

At the end of the courtyard a stairway of 41 steps descends into a huge cellar of the early 13th century, divided into three ogival vaulted naves by twelve pillars with foliated capitals. It is one of the most remarkable secular buildings of that era remaining in France. Suitably, the floor was originally made of beaten earth. To the right, at the entrance, a pedestal is sculpted as a beery face, indeed a good archetype of caricature.

OLD CHARTRES.
THE BANKS OF THE EURE. VIEWS.

The stroller will enjoy exploring the maze of old streets in Chartres, which still carry racy names steeped in the past : names of crafts and signs for the most part. These tours are only worth doing on foot. The lower town is recommended during the morning when bathed in sunlight. From the banks of the Eure and its old bridges a good view can be had of the Cathedral. The best are those from the Bouju bridge, from the Rue de la Porte-Guillaume, and from the bridge of Saint-Hilaire.

Towards the circular boulevards there are likewise fine views from the Courtille bridge, the Guillaume Gate (which takes its name from Vidame Guillaume de Ferrières) and from the New Bridge. Lastly, one should not miss the panorama of the town from the eastern slope (Avenue Neigre or Rue d'Aboville for example) or the public garden running along the road leading out to Paris. The preservation of old Chartres is the object of careful attention (urban architect : Guy Nicot). The town Chartres conceals here and there old houses and mansions of various periods. Attention should be drawn to its churches ; Saint-Pierre is of special interest and importance.. The sightseer will wish to visit Saint-Martin-au-Val also, with its pre-romanesque crypt, the ancient church of Saint-André, almost entirely romanesque, and Saint-Aignan, rich in Renaissance detail.

THE CHURCH OF SAINT-PIERRE.

The church of Saint-Pierre was, until the revolutionary era, the Abbey of the Benedictines of Saint-Père-en-Vallée ; it had been settled anew during the 10th c. by monks coming from Saint Benoît de Fleury, nowadays Saint-Benoît-sur-Loire. It is not only the most remarkable monument in the town after the Cathedral, but one of the most worthy of interest of French churches, on account of its architecture — in particular the daring conception of the choir, an excellent example of the "radiant" style — and above all the stained glass, the quantity and quality of which, as an example of the art of stained glass of about 1300, is a collection without equal in France, or elsewhere.

The 7th century Abbey of Saint-Père received a donation from Saint Bathilde, the wife of Clovis II. After a series of disasters it was rebuilt, and towards the end of the 10th century, as the Abbey was beyond the town walls and in a position of vulnerability in the valley, the Count and the Abbot begged King Hugues Capet to be allowed to erect suitable defences. It is likely that the bell-tower-keep of the church dates from this period.

During the great fire of 1134 which ravaged the whole town, Saint-Père-en-Vallée suffered considerable damage. The monk Hilduard organised building of a new choir between 1151 an 1165, the lower floors of which, together with the ambulatory and chapels, remain. In digging the foundations of a provisional wall to enclose the building yard, the tomb was found of Gilduin, a young deacon of 24 who came to Chartres on pilgrimage and died at Saint-Père in 1077. Elected Bishop of Dol against his wish, he was returning from Rome, where the Pope had accepted his refusal on account of his extreme youth. So many of the faithful flowed to the tomb of Saint Gilduin, officially honoured in 1165, that the gifts left by them enabled work to continue on the Abbey in an imposing style.

A little before 1200 they started on the north side of the nave, then in the 13th century they commenced the south side, the pillars of which are related to those of the Cathedral. During the reign of Saint Louis, on the huge piers of Hilduard's choir, was thrown a framework of stone of extraordinary lightness; glasswork occupies the maximum surface, and the triforium itself is a clerestory.

A homogeneous collection of glass embellishes the upper floors; several of which in the nave can be dated with certainty to the years 1307-1315. The iconographic programme is masterfully composed, and at the same time the problem of lighting was skillfully resolved. In the nave, the bays in grisaille with characters in colours alternate with historiated compositions. The north is set aside for Saint John the Baptist and the Apostles; the south for other saints in order of the hierarchy; monks, bishops, and popes. In the last bays of the nave, one of the historiated windows is dedicated to the Virgin, and the other to Christ.

In the four Lancets of the Choir windows Patriarchs and Prophets alternate with vertical bands of ornamental grisaille. In the centre, the glass dazzles with its reds and blues, in which symmetry is avoided. Here are seen Apostles, Martyrs and Confessors. The two Lancets of the axis are occupied by the Virgin on a blue background, and the Crucifixion on a red one. Below, Saint Louis, haloed, is next to Saint Gilduin, dressed as a deacon, pushing away a crozier very discreetly shown near the edge.

MUSÉE 71. ZURBARAN : SAINTE LUCIE
72. VIERGE A L'ENFANT

75

76. CELLIER DE LOENS
77. L'ÉGLISE SAINT-ANDRÉ
VUE DU PONT DES MINIMES
78. L'EURE AU PONT DE LA
COURTILLE. SAINT-PIERRE
ET SAINT-AIGNAN

79

80

81

82

83

84

79 à 82. CHAPITEAUX DE LA CRYPTE
DE SAINT-MARTIN-AU-VAL
83. MAISON ROMANE
84. MAISON DU SAUMON

85
86

With the suppleness and virility of its design, by the bold distribution of its splashes of colour, the stained glass of Saint Pierre occupies a high place in French art. Note the rich effects obtained with limited means : movements and expressions are reduced to essentials, and often in the larger figures the same sketch is used for two people, but the colours of their clothes are subtly reversed.

Fine fragments of Renaissance stained glass are found in the triforium. They belonged to the parochial church of Saint-Hilaire, which, before the Revolution, stood nearby. Some of them are attributed to Robert Pinaigrier.

In the chapel of the chevet are the tombstone of Simon de Bérou, and the Virgin sculpted by Bridan for the episcopal chapel (18th century).

The two isolated piers of the Saint-Soline Chapel, to the South, serve as relievers to the double-vaulted flying buttresses which rest on the abbatial structure. There, near the burial place of Mgr. Harscouet († 1954) are exposed the relics of Saint Gilduin, rediscovered in 1944 after the bombardment of the Church of Champhol, where they had lain almost forgotten since the Revolution. Here are modern statues of Saint Gilduin, by Cappabianca, and Saint Fulbert, by Jean Galopin. Saint Fulbert († 1028) was interred in the Abbey.

The windows of the south side aisle, glazed in pasticcio, start above the cloister, therefore their dimensions are smaller than those on the north side.

The small 13th century portal merits attention, but more so the play of the flying buttresses, particularly graceful at the apse. In the upper part of the lateral windows of the choir, circular and octagonal roses alternate. Flanking the south side of the chevet is a light turret audaciously supported by the ambulatory vault. It can be seen from the Rue de l'Ane-Rez, as can the Abbatial buildings, reconstructed between 1700 and 1709.

SAINT-ANDRÉ.

The ancient collegial church of Saint-André, dating in parts from the 11th century was rebuilt after the fire of 1134 which had seriously damaged it. Secularised during the Revolution it has since then undergone two ravages by fire : in 1861 and 1944. The choir no longer exists. It daringly jutted over the Eure on an arch thrown over from one bank to the other, the beginning of which is still visible.

It was in the 12th century that the façade was built. The portal capitals, amongst the most finely chiselled of the Romanesque period (about 1140) are embellished with figures mingled with plant motives. The upper floor dates from about 1180. The tower, formerly topped by a wooden spire, dominates the Close, which was the Cemetery of the Innocents.

88. RUE DES ÉCUYERS

Flanked by side aisles, the huge nave gives the impression of power; more arresting perhaps because of the damage caused to it by the fire. On the southern side the only break in the rhythm of the large cylindrical columns is caused by the bulk of one which contains the steps by which the pulpit was reached. The building was never vaulted, but had an ordinary visible roof; only in the bay of the bell-tower is there a groined vault. In the transept are seen the joins of the aisles of the choir, added during the Renaissance.

To the north, the Saint-Ignace Chapel, of the early 16th century, is still flamboyant in its fenestration, but Renaissance in the piers which support its ridge-ribbed vault. Jean de Beauce, perhaps its architect, was interred in Saint-André, but the exact position of his burial place is uncertain.

Low doors in the side aisles open onto steps leading to the crypt, pre-12th century. The ground level is only just above the Eure, and steps, more or less submerged, depending on the season, lead down from the southern bay.

THE CHURCH OF SAINT-AIGNAN.

Founded, it is believed, about the year 400, by Saint-Aignan bishop of Chartres, the parish later on took the name of its founder. It is the oldest in the town, and was that of the Counts, whose château was quite near.

The reconstruction of the present church took place towards the beginning of the 16th century. Not until the following century was it completed, but on a more modest scale than was originally conceived : the buttresses never received the abutment-piers which were designed for them. Only one was built, which supported the turret of the façade. The cluster of columns on the interior, raised to receive ogival vaulting, serve only to hold up the visible timber roof.

Begun in the last gothic period, the building contains many, Renaissance elements. In 1850 they built into the centre of the façade a 14th century portal which formerly stood nearby but only opened into a blind alley. The side entrance, dating from 1541, particularly well-finished in its decoration, had always taken the place of the principal entrance.

The tower of fluted pilasters was cut short and topped by a simple wooden belfrey. The chevet can best be appreciated from the Rue Saint-Pierre : it is perched on the edge of the ramparts of the upper town; the base of the choir is a well lit crypt in the flamboyant style.

The main nave surprisingly has polychrome decoration, which it was felt necessary to give it during the last century. The gallery, in the "antique style" of 1625, takes the form of a triforium. The same date is inscribed above the choir, on one of the tie-beams supporting the shingle board of decorated wood.

The side aisles with ribbed vaults have blazoned keystones. The vault near to the southern façade is sculpted with skulls; as a matter of fact the side door, called "des Morts", had direct access to the parochial cemetery.

Amongst many sumptuous Renaissance vaults, notice that of the Saint Michel Chapel (1543) on the south side.

Saint-Aignan retains only a little of its collection of 16th century stained glass; the explosion of a canon, set in position in the nearby cemetery during the siege of 1568, shattered numerous panels. In two windows near the entrance fragments have been re-assembled as a puzzle. After the third stained-glass window, called "The Bishops" (Saints Martin, Denis, Aignan, and Nicholas), that of the Dormition, Funeral, and Coronation of Our Lady, is without doubt the most noteworthy. To the south there is the curious window of Saint Michel (in the Chapel of the same name) by the glass-maker Jean Jouan (1547) who was inspired by Raphael and Dürer. Many beautiful old panels can be seen in the southern side aisles.

The glazing in the ambulatory are copies. On the south side one large window, and many smaller ones, contain modern glass.

SAINT-MARTIN-AU-VAL.

The ancient church of Saint-Martin-au-Val today serves as a Chapel for the Hospice Saint Brice (reach it via the Rue des Bas-Bourgs, for preference). Although the building was the object of radical restoration in 1865, and although its façade, flanked by two turrets, is not original, the whole retains its romanesque volume and an exceptional unity of plan although the nave has been shortened. One reaches the transept by a small interior courtyard surrounded by 17th century buildings, in which traces of a cloister are evident.

The interior stuns by its size, and the effective setting of its heightened choir. A shingle covers the whole. Of the twin capitals of the crossing exhibiting interwoven designs and monsters, four only are authentic.

At the base of the nave, the holy-water basin is hewn from a white marble Roman capital. In the north transept is the tomb and recumbant figure of Mgr. Clausel de Montals, by Fromanger (1853), and an 18th century lectern. Against the north base of the choir, in the ambulatory, is a romanesque arcade with a polychrome frieze.

The **crypt**, placed under the choir, is one of exceptional interest. It is entered from the south side. Above the door can be seen a fragment of a gallo-roman wall with a herring-bone pattern. The crypt, reconstructed towards the end of the 10th century, contains much material of an earlier date : well-proportioned monolithic shafts hewn in rare stone, with bases decorated by cable-moulding and capitals diversely treated. One of these, to the right of the altar, is related to the Corinthian style, and shows many analogies with certain capitals at Jouarre. Its neighbour, of unusual type, is possibly merovingian. If those of the hemicycle display the usual romanesque subjects, the two of the west partition are remarkable for their primitive features. Their themes could be Peace or Love opposed to Violence.

Saint-Martin-au-Val is, apart from the Cathedral, the oldest sanctuary in Chartres. A gallo-roman cemetery occupies its immediate approaches, and close by the first Christian sepulchres, an oratory, which was the origin of the monastery, was built. The latter from the earliest times took the name of Saint Martin de Tours. Cited in 10th century texts, it was dependent on Marmoutier until 1663. Jacques du Terrail, brother of Bayard, was its Prior in 1529.

The four primitive sarcophagi in the crypt contained, it is believed, the bodies of bishops of Chartres who died in the 6th century. Crosses in relief decorate them.

By tradition each new bishop of Chartres solemnly enters his episcopal town only after a night's vigil of prayer at Saint-Martin-au-Val.

OLD MANSIONS, HOUSES, AND OTHER MONUMENTS.

A good number of streets are bordered by old houses, for example the Rue du Cheval-Blanc, near the Cathedral, with its overhanging gables, and one (17B) of brick with wooden braces.

Steps, called "tertres", and steep streets descend towards the lower town. One of the most picturesque, the Rue Chantault, has in it doors and windows of every age. Its 12th century **romanesque house** (No. 29) exhibiting on its tympanum strange sculptures, is one of the oldest in France. In this district, near the Pont du Massacre, the **Chapel of Notre Dame de la Brèche** contains the old Virgin of the Drouaise Gate, and cannon balls of the 1568 siege.

The **Staircase of Queen Berthe** (35 Rue des Ecuyers) is a turret stair showing sculpted plaster work of the early 16th century. Located near the foot of the old castle, it reminds one with its name, of Berthe, who when window of the Count of Chartres, Eudes I, married Robert II, King of France. The picturesque "rue des Ecuyers" is lined with some half-timbered houses.

The **House of the Salmon** (12 place de la Poissonnerie) dates from the 15th century. On its consoles, a huge salmon and an Annunciation can be seen; and also curious snails on a vine. To the right, under the second floor, the Spinning Sow, encumbered by distaff and spindle.

The **Maison Huvé** (10 Rue Noël-Ballay) has an ornate Renaissance façade, with columns, pediments, and caryatids, and was built about 1550 by doctor Claude Huvé, a humanist with an eye for beauty, as the inscription on the cartouche gives us to understand.

Notice in front of the Old Church of Saint Foy, 16th century (with a restored exterior) its romanesque doorway (12th century) isolated today; nearby is the **monument to Jean Moulin,** and at the entrance of the Rue Collin d'Harleville, facing the Prefecture, an old door of a gambling-den of the time of Francis 1st: the **Hotel de Champrond** (26 Place Jean-Moulin) with its basket-handle doorway; a house with sculpted consoles (16th century) at 20 Rue Porte-Morard; the façade of the old Carmelite Chapel (17th century) now rue Sainte-Thérèse; a mansion of the late gothic period at 12 Rue de Grenets, and at No. 11, opposite, a Renaissance doorway; and a huge plaster-work gable in the Place de l'Etape-au-Vin.

Close by, the **Hotel Montescot,** an old residence in the Henri IV style, became the town-hall in 1792. Built by Clause de Montescot, it was completed in 1614. On the pediment, above the doors, are busts (restored) of Henri IV, Louis XIII, and Marie de Medicis. Inside there is a formal staircase with a rampant vault. Enlarged by the addition of a modern wing, (the architect was Jean Maunoury) the main façade of the town hall (1960) now faces the Place des Halles. On a background of Berchère stone, shown to advantage by large surfaces of glass, stands out in ironwork the secular coat of arms of Chartres, three fleurs de lis and three bezants.

The reception room is embellished by Bouchot's masterpiece : **The Removal of Marceau, mortally wounded.**

Chartres, which is continuously developing, takes pride in its Charter of Freedom, signed in 1297, which is kept in the Town Hall.

ENVIRONS.

Beyond the Close of Saint-Jean, a public garden laid out on the site of an abbey razed to the ground during the religious wars, the Rechèvres district possesses the interesting modern church of Saint Jean-Baptiste (1961) built by the generosity of German catholics who had been prisoners of war in Chartres, (Jean Redreau, Architect, stained glass by Max Ingrand). The church houses the tomb of Franz Stock "the almoner of hell" of the years of occupation.

Not far from the Place Drouais is a charming public park called the "Horticultural Garden". In the same direction, the suburb of Lèves occupies a rural site. Its modern church (1956) is noteworthy (A. L. Pinchon, Architect, stained glass by G. Loire, sculptures by Lembert-Rucki and Marc Jaquin, altar by André Martin, and ironwork by René Birard). Nearby, the Aligre Home, which replaces the original Abbey of Josephat, exhibits a lapidary museum in its 14th century cloister, and near the ruins of the romanesque church can be seen the sculpted sarcophagus of John of Salisbury († 1180).

One of the most enjoyable walks in the neighbourhood is the Eure Valley. There, one comes across smiling villages, water-mills, dolmens, and churches full of character, particularly that of Saint-Piat.

Only twelve miles from Chartres, the Château of Maintenon, a pleasant building in which feudal architecture is associated with that of a country house, welcomes visitors into its apartments, still full of souvenirs of Louis XIV and Madame de Maintenon. In the park where Racine mused upon Esther, the mirrors of water, formed by the confluence of the Eure and Voise, reflect Vauban's aqueducts, destined to feed the ornamental lakes of Versailles. Left unfinished, it has the noble air of a roman ruin, and adds to the charm of the landscape.

Between the Seine and Loire, at the junction of the vast lands of Beauce with its flat horizons, and the pleasant evergreen undulations of Perche, which is extended by Thimerais and Drouais, with their forests, this countryside of contrasts is enriched by a collection of monuments of all ages; churches, hardly known, such as Gallardon, Dreux, Bonneval and Nogent le Roi; châteaux also, some of which enjoy renown, such as Anet, on the boundary of the Ile de France and Normandy, and Châteaudun, already belonging to the great family of the Châteaux of the Loire.

Printed off on 20th June 1975
by SCOP SADAG, 01201 Bellegarde.
The first edition of this book
was published in 1963.
Legally deposited : first quarter 1963.
N^o of edition 931   N^o of printing 1 179
Printed in France